DATE DUE

HO CHI MINH

Essential Lives

Ho Chi Minh

NORTH VIETNAMESE PRESIDENT

by Kristin F. Johnson

Content Consultant: Clarence R. Wyatt,
Pottinger Professor of History and Special Assistant to the President,
Centre College

ABDO
Publishing Company

CREDITS

Published by ABDO Publishing Company, 8000 West 78th Street, Edina, Minnesota 55439. Copyright © 2012 by Abdo Consulting Group, Inc. International copyrights reserved in all countries. No part of this book may be reproduced in any form without written permission from the publisher. The Essential Library™ is a trademark and logo of ABDO Publishing Company.

Printed in the United States of America,
North Mankato, Minnesota
062011
092011

 THIS BOOK CONTAINS AT LEAST 10% RECYCLED MATERIALS.

Editor: Mari Kesselring
Copy Editor: Rebecca Rowell
Cover Design: Kazuko Collins
Interior Design and Production: Marie Tupy

Library of Congress Cataloging-in-Publication Data
Johnson, Kristin F., 1968-
  Ho Chi Minh : North Vietnamese president / by Kristin F. Johnson.
    p. cm. -- (Essential lives)
  Includes bibliographical references.
  ISBN 978-1-61783-006-8
  1. Ho, Chi Minh, 1890-1969--Juvenile literature. 2. Presidents--Vietnam (Democratic Republic)--Biography--Juvenile literature. 3. Vietnam (Democratic Republic)--History--Juvenile literature. 4. Vietnam (Democratic Republic)--Biography--Juvenile literature. I. Title.
  DS560.72.H6J64 2012
  959.7'304092--dc22
  [B]
                                        2011015334

TABLE OF CONTENTS

*Ho Chi Minh announcing both his presidency
and his intent for Vietnam independence, September 2, 1945*

FIGHT FOR INDEPENDENCE

On September 2, 1945, just after 2:00 p.m., a thin, frail man stepped out of the shadows and onto a platform in front of thousands of people in Ba Dinh Square. One source reported that approximately 500,000 people gathered in the crowded square in Hanoi, Vietnam. Dressed in a humble khaki suit and sandals, the man looked out at the crowd. His long, wispy beard flowed in the wind. The man was Ho Chi Minh.

"All men are created equal," Ho began. "They are endowed by their Creator with certain unalienable Rights; among these are Life, Liberty, and the pursuit of Happiness."[1] Ho remembered reading these opening words in the US Declaration of Independence. And with these words, Ho quickly captivated the large audience. Some historians have speculated that Ho included this language to gain support from the United States for his cause of independence for Vietnam. However, because the United States feared the spread of communism, that support would not materialize.

Ho continued his speech with words from France's Declaration of the Rights of Man and Citizen: "All men are born free and with equal rights," he said, "and must always remain free and have equal rights."[2]

Vietnamese Names

The order of Vietnamese names has special significance. The family name is listed first, then the middle name, followed by given names. The Vietnamese have very few family names, so most people are not known by their family name. Instead, they are called by their given names. This, however, was not the case with Ho Chi Minh. In rare instances, a person is called by his or her family name to show tremendous respect. This level of respect is why Ho was often called President Ho or Uncle Ho by his people.

With this statement, Ho was making a point that the French, who had colonized Vietnam and oppressed the Vietnamese—his people—were hypocrites for going against their own stated principles.

Ho had delivered many speeches during his lifetime, but this was his most important. He was announcing his presidency and officially declaring Vietnamese independence. With this very public announcement, Ho was also risking his life by taking on his country's enemies. This was his first public appearance after being away from Vietnam for 30 years. During this time away, he traveled using many different aliases to avoid being caught for his subversive activities. Still, he was jailed twice for revolutionary acts and alliances. Many people believed Ho was dead, so when the 55-year-old revolutionary walked out onto the stage that September, he surprised many.

Who Is Ho Chi Minh?

Though Ho became president of North Vietnam and was a well-known figure, his life was shrouded

Confucius

Ho is sometimes described as a combination of a Confucian philosopher and Marxist revolutionary. Confucius was a Chinese philosopher who lived from 551 BCE to 479 BCE. He taught moral principles, including how governments should treat their people and how people should treat one another. Confucius is credited with the earliest version of the Golden Rule: "Do not do to others what you do not want done to yourself."[3] Ho was known to quote this phrase often.

in mystery. But it is known that Ho advocated for a specific cause: unifying Vietnam and freeing the Vietnamese from colonial rule at all costs. Ho often said, "Nothing is more precious than independence and liberty."[4] Ho was willing to use violence to free his country from colonial rule.

A Colonized Country

Colonizers, including the Chinese, the French, and the Japanese, had occupied Vietnam for centuries. Vietnam was attractive as a colony because of its fertile crops and location bordering the coast of the South China Sea. Colonizers could profit from the country's resources.

Why Colonize Vietnam?

The French government's rule of Indochina began in the mid-nineteenth century. The French declared themselves a protector, watching over the smaller, weaker Vietnam and its neighboring countries. But the French government oppressed the Vietnamese to keep them from retaliating under French control.

One reason the French wanted to occupy Vietnam was the attractive location of the country, right on the border of Asia. This was an optimal spot for ease of importing and exporting goods. Vietnam was rich with rice, rubber, tea, and coal products, so controlling these resources made the French wealthy. Additionally, Vietnam had a key river that allowed the French to send boats through the Indochinese countries to China. Another reason to occupy Vietnam was competition. France wanted to prevent Great Britain, one of its key rivals, from gaining this stronghold in Asia.

While Ho was growing up in the late nineteenth and early twentieth centuries, the French occupied Vietnam. The French government had begun ruling Indochina in the mid-nineteenth century. French Indochina had been officially established in 1887. Indochina consisted of Cambodia, Laos, and Vietnam. To better control the Vietnamese people, the French split Vietnam into three regions: Cochin China, Annam, and Tonkin. The Vietnamese wanted independence from the French, who forced them to labor and stripped the land of its economic resources.

Other Enemies

By 1945, the Vietnamese had a new enemy ruler. The French lost control of Vietnam to the Japanese. But under the leadership of Ho and his compatriots, the Vietnamese held more effective uprisings to fight for their independence. These uprisings lasted for many years, even though Japan's troops far outnumbered Ho's troops. Despite the military disadvantage of the Vietnamese, they often succeeded in defeating their colonizers and other enemies.

Later, the Vietnamese would also fight the United States in the Vietnam War. However, over the course of the revolution and the Vietnam War with the United

*President Ho Chi Minh, center,
visiting antiaircraft fighters during the Vietnam War, 1966*

States, many people died because of Ho's unwillingness to negotiate a peace settlement. Over the 30 years of war that followed Ho's speech, many people perished, including approximately 4 million Vietnamese, more than 75,000 French, and approximately 58,000 US soldiers. Ho would settle for nothing less than complete independence for Vietnam.

Honored and Feared

The Vietnamese people honored and feared Ho. They also saw him as being like them. Even as president of North Vietnam, Ho remained humble. He often dressed in a simple white tunic and homemade rubber sandals, which was a common style of dress for Vietnamese men.

Ho had a persuasive and calm manner unlike the approach of other leaders of the time, such as Russian leader Vladimir Lenin, Soviet ruler Joseph Stalin, and German dictator Adolf Hitler, who were known for their strong personalities and for giving thunderous speeches. Ho was more subtle and understated, yet he was well-respected. He earned this respect and the name Uncle Ho because he spent his entire life fighting for independence for his homeland.

The day Ho appeared in public to declare independence changed the course of not only Vietnamese history, but also the history for many other people suffering from colonial oppression. This simple man, with his quiet and grandfatherly manner, was about to rise up and become the legendary Ho Chi Minh. ⌐

Poor Conditions for the Vietnamese

The French forced Vietnamese peasants to harvest the rich rice crops produced in the fertile Mekong delta area. The French then exported most of the rice, leaving many Vietnamese to starve. During French colonial rule, Indochina became the third-largest exporter in the world for rice. This achievement helped make the French wealthy while leaving the Vietnamese to become even poorer. The peasants were also made to build new roads and buildings. Many workers died from being overworked, contracting diseases such as malaria, or suffering from malnutrition.

*Before, during, and after his presidency,
the people of Vietnam held Ho in great respect.*

Cung's family home during childhood
was a traditional Vietnamese hut made of straw.

REVOLUTIONARY START

o was born Nguyen Sinh Cung on May 19,
1890, in the small village of Kim Lien.
Located in the Annam region of Vietnam, the
village was surrounded by mountains on one side
and the sea on the other. Because of the terrain and

the humid climate, the villagers were subjected to droughts and flooding. They were always prepared for the worst conditions, such as crop failures and food shortages. As a result, the people were poor and frugal with their food. They planned ahead for problematic conditions.

Cung and his family lived in a three-room straw hut. It was located on a small plot of land approximately one-half acre (.2 ha) in size. The family farmed this land and lived off what they produced. Their village was known for its anticolonial sentiment, so it is not surprising that Cung would later become a revolutionary.

A Revolutionary Education

Cung was the youngest of three children. The oldest was his sister, Nguyen Thi Thanh, and the middle child was his brother, Nguyen Sinh Khiem. Cung's father, Nguyen Sinh Sac, had been orphaned at the age of four. Sac had been adopted by a scholar who encouraged him to pursue education. When Sac grew up, he worked as a teacher. In 1894, Sac took the civil service examinations. He earned the level of *cu nhan*, which is similar to earning a master of arts degree in the United States. Sac continued teaching in Kim Lien but later moved the family to Hué. There, he would take more difficult exams.

In 1900, Sac was appointed to a government position that required him to move. He took Khiem, his older son, with him and left the rest of the family in Hué. While living in Hué, Cung's mother, Hoang Thi Loan, gave birth to a fourth child, another son. But Loan soon became ill. She died on February 10, 1901. The fourth child also became ill and died when he was only one year old.

After this, Sac moved the last of the family back to Kim Lien. In 1901, he took the civil service examinations again and was awarded a higher honor, *pho bang*, which he could have used to further his career. Instead, Sac built a school in the village and stayed there teaching the classics. He also gave money to the poor, which kept his family living very modestly. This made an impression upon

Importance of Education

Sac always encouraged education. He even posted a plaque on a wall of his family's home that read "Good studies will lift you out of poverty."[1]

Thanh's father, who built a schoolhouse in their hometown village, taught Thanh the importance of education.

Cung, teaching him to sacrifice for the common good.

When Cung was 11, his father renamed him Nguyen Tat Thanh, which means "Nguyen Who Will Be Victorious." This name change followed Vietnamese tradition. A new name is chosen to reflect the parents' hopes for the child's future. Sac clearly wanted his son to have a successful life.

Thanh's schooling consisted of classroom teachings, but he also learned from friends of his father who were well versed in Confucian teachings and the history of the Vietnamese people. Like his father, Thanh did well in school. He studied *quoc-ngu*, the romanized Vietnamese alphabet, as well as French. Learning French was important, as one of his tutors had said, "If you want to defeat the French, you must understand them. To understand the French, you must study the French language."[2]

The Language

The current Vietnamese written alphabet is referred to as *quoc-ngu*, which means "national language." It was developed by Portuguese missionaries who used the new language to translate Vietnamese writings for teaching purposes. The new alphabet originated from Latin characters instead of keeping the traditional Chinese symbols the Vietnamese had originally used to communicate in writing.

Quoc-ngu was taught in schools. Thanh learned it in his early studies at the National Academy in Hué. In addition to its Latin characters, the alphabet has accent marks to indicate how a word should sound and the tone people should use when reading the sound. These accent marks are called diacritics. Some letters have multiple diacritics. This Romanized writing form was also much simpler for the Vietnamese to learn than the former Chinese symbols or ideograms had been. Quoc-ngu became the official national language in 1919.

Thanh's classmates remembered him as a hard worker who would often continue studying while they played. Thanh often said, "Only through hardship can we succeed."[3] Thanh's hard work showed when he finished a two-year course of study in one year.

Young Revolutionary

In 1906, Sac accepted another government appointment and moved with Thanh and Khiem to Hué to work, while his daughter stayed behind in Kim Lien. In 1907, Thanh and his brother entered the Quoc Hoc, or National Academy, after passing the entrance exams. Though the school was prestigious, its building was run-down. The roof leaked when it rained. At the school, Thanh sometimes got into fights because he was teased for his regional accent. Still, Thanh did well in school, mostly because of his language skills.

Soon, Thanh began speaking out against the government. This got him in trouble with school officials. In May 1908, tensions in Hué grew as peasants protested high taxes. Thanh joined the protests. The demonstrations turned violent as police pushed protestors and even

Early Praise for a Good Student

Thanh was a dedicated student praised early on by his teachers for his hard work. When he was studying French in school, his teacher Mr. Queinnec wrote the following comment on one of Thanh's papers: "Thanh wrote his paper on the writing of verse; he is an intelligent and very distinguished student."[4]

struck some with batons, including Thanh. Thanh then acted as an interpreter between the Vietnamese peasants and French government officials. This put him at the heart of the conflict. But the next day, because of his participation in the protest, officials pulled Thanh from his classroom and expelled him from school. Thanh was earning a reputation as an agitator.

WORKING HIS WAY WEST

After being dismissed from school at the age of 18, Thanh moved south to look for work. He could not go home because officials were watching him. He was afraid he would be arrested or would put his family in danger. In fact, surveillance surrounded his whole family on revolutionary suspicions. Thanh's siblings had also spoken out against the colonial government. Since the government had blacklisted his name, it was difficult for Thanh to find work. He eventually found a job as a teaching assistant in the small fishing village of Phan Thiet.

While in Phan Thiet, a typhoon struck and damaged the port. Thanh watched in horror as his countrymen were ordered by French officials to dive into the dangerous waters and salvage what they could from the destroyed ships. Many of the dockworkers died in these attempts. A stunned Thanh looked on as the French appeared amused by the ordeal. The incident added to Thanh's anger toward the colonialists.

HARD TIMES FOR THANH'S FATHER

Meanwhile, Sac was working as a judge who decided the fate of criminals. Sac started giving out harsher, atypical punishments, and he was also known to drink in excess. Sac felt his work was not worthwhile. In January 1910, Sac sentenced one man to 100 lashes with a cane. The man died two months later, and the man's family complained about Sac's harsh treatment. Sac was convicted of being too brutal. He was caned himself and eventually dismissed from his job. Sac was too ashamed to return to Kim Lien, so he moved to Saigon. There, he worked as an

Caning

Caning is a form of judicial corporal punishment used in many Asian countries as a standard punishment. Caning consists of hitting the guilty person with a stick or cane, generally on the person's buttocks or hands. This punishment is also common in schools, where teachers administer it. Countries in Africa and the Middle East also use caning.

herbalist and taught Chinese. In his disappointment, Sac remarked, "When the country is lost, how can you have a home."[5] Thanh never forgot these words.

Thanh was affected in another way. His father's damaged reputation made it difficult for Thanh to find work. So, he made his way to Saigon, the largest port for ships leaving the country. In 1911, Thanh applied for a position working on a French passenger ship as a chef's helper, saying in the interview that he could do anything. He got the job, and it would soon allow 21-year-old Thanh to leave Vietnam.

*A young Thanh set off to see the world
and gather knowledge from other cultures.*

While working aboard a ship, Thanh visited places such as Marseilles, France, studying their language and government.

SEEING THE WORLD

*G*etting the job aboard the ship, named *Amiral Latouche-Tréville*, provided Thanh the perfect opportunity to leave Vietnam and see the world. Thanh wanted to see how well Western democracies worked. He hoped to bring the ideas behind those governments, as well as independence, to his people in Vietnam.

Life at Sea

On the first part of his journey abroad, Thanh worked for several weeks on the ship as a chef's helper. Thanh's daily chores began at 4:00 a.m. and included cleaning the kitchen, lighting boilers, and carrying heavy loads of coal and food. In the evenings, after chores were completed around 9:00 p.m., Thanh continued studying French and also English. These languages would be useful when he became a political propagandist. Later in life, he was fluent in these languages and also in Chinese, German, and Russian. On the ship, Thanh also read extensively, including authors Leo Tolstoy, William Shakespeare, Émile Zola, and Karl Marx.

During the journey, the ship docked in several ports. This allowed Thanh to see many lands, including other parts of Asia, Africa, Europe, and Latin America. On July 6, 1911, the ship stopped in Marseilles, France, giving Thanh his first look at the country that was oppressing his people. There, Thanh recalled being addressed respectfully by the French when he stopped for coffee at a café. For the first

time in his life, he was called "monsieur."[1] During
the visit, Thanh noted a similarity between France
and Indochina: they both had poverty. Additionally,
he witnessed that France had its own uncivilized
people, such as thieves, prostitutes, and the homeless.
The French had claimed that in colonizing, they were
civilizing those types of people in Indochina. Seeing
these problems on the streets of Marseilles, Thanh
wondered to himself, "Why don't the French civilize
their compatriots before doing it to us?"[2]

VISITING PROGRESSIVE NATIONS

Thanh continued his travels aboard the *Amiral
Latouche-Tréville*, which included going to the United
States. In 1913, he left the ship after it made port
in New York, New York. The time he spent in the
United States is unclear, but he is believed to have lived
and worked in New York City's Harlem neighborhood.
Though Thanh was reportedly impressed by the
apparent equality afforded to Asians there, he was
shocked by the racism against black people in the United
States. The United States claimed to value democracy
and freedom, but it did not grant such rights to all
of its people. This proved to Thanh that Western,
democratic ways left much room for improvement.

Thanh wrote a vivid article about lynching in the United States. There is speculation, however, that he only read about lynching and did not observe the events firsthand. Lynching usually took place in the South, far from where he lived in New York City. In the article, published in *La Correspondance Internationale*, a Russian Communist periodical that was printed in several languages, Thanh explicitly detailed the barbarous acts of some whites against blacks. He wrote, "[T]he black race is the most oppressed and most exploited of the human family."[3]

> "The people of Vietnam, including my own father, often wondered who would help them to remove the yoke of French control. Some said Japan, others Great Britain, and some said the United States. I saw that I must go abroad to see for myself. After I had found out how they lived, I would return to help my countrymen."[4]
>
> —*Ho Chi Minh*

LIVING IN LONDON

After leaving the United States around 1913, Thanh settled in London, England. He worked as a snow sweeper and then as a boiler operator. Thanh eventually left these jobs because of the grueling work and poor conditions. After this, he worked for the famous chef Auguste Escoffier in the Drayton Hotel. It was reported that Thanh saved scraps discarded by patrons and gave them to the poor. This act of kindness impressed Escoffier, who promoted Thanh from washing dishes to making cakes. Inequality in labor practices in London, however, prompted Thanh and other Asian workers in London to organize the Overseas Workers' Association. The association's goal was to improve the rights and working conditions of Asian workers who were not allowed to join the British trade unions. This was one of Thanh's earliest involvements in politics.

In December 1917, Thanh reportedly returned to France, though this date is often disputed because the French authorities did not start tracking his actions until 1919. When Thanh arrived in Paris in 1917, he officially changed his name again. Nguyen Tat Thanh became Nguyen Ai Quoc, or "Nguyen the Patriot." He lived and worked in Paris for two years without the government taking an interest in him.

Reports speculate that Quoc went to Paris to continue working for Vietnamese independence. Many Vietnamese people had recently moved

Thanh, the Patient Revolutionary

As Nguyen Tat Thanh, he wrote a letter to his scholar friend Phan Chu Trinh in 1914 after World War I began. The text shows Thanh's patience in waiting for the right time for revolution:

"Gunfire rings out through the air and corpses cover the ground. Five great powers are engaged in battle. Nine countries are at war. . . . I think that in the next three or four months the destiny of Asia will change dramatically. Too bad for those who are fighting and struggling. We just have to remain calm."[5]

The world's leaders attended the Paris Peace Conference in 1919, including US President Woodrow Wilson, far right, whom Quoc hoped to impress.

to Paris. In one biography, author Pierre Brocheux reported that "between 1915 and 1919, there were 49,180 Indochinese workers and 42,922 Indochinese infantrymen, and an equal number of Chinese workers and student workers present in Europe, studying or working at the front lines of northern France."[6]

EIGHT-POINT PLAN FOR PEACE

Fellow Vietnamese revolutionaries elected Quoc to represent them at the 1919 Paris Peace Conference.

The goal of the conference was for the nations involved in World War I (1914–1918) to sign postwar conditions for peace. Quoc wanted to appear impressive to US President Woodrow Wilson, so he rented a suit and a bowler, which was the fashion for hats of that time. Quoc believed the US president would be sympathetic to the plight of the Vietnamese and their will to live as an independent country since the United States had struggled to gain freedom from England and become a democracy. Wilson had also made statements about decolonization in his Fourteen Points plan. These statements made Quoc believe that Wilson might be sympathetic to the Vietnamese cause.

But Quoc was not the only representative there from a small country waiting to plead his case for help from the United States. Wilson politely turned down meetings with Quoc and all of the other country representatives.

Quoc's involvement in the conference caught the attention of French authorities. Quoc confused the police because they had no records of a Nguyen Ai Quoc in their immigration logs, so the police watched him. Quoc quickly became labeled as an agitator because he lobbied French newspapers and politicians to make the Vietnamese colonial problem known. Quoc made demands of the French government in a document called "The Demands of the Vietnamese People." The document was a simple plan with eight points for an independent Vietnam.

After the conference, Quoc was more determined than ever to fight for the independence of his small nation. Next, he turned to the Communists to learn how to incite a revolution. If diplomacy and talking

Eight-Point Plan for Peace

Quoc's eight-point plan was written in French and sent to French newspapers in 1919. There is debate about who actually wrote the document, though Quoc took credit for writing it. Quoc was not fluent in French at the time, so he may have had help from his close colleague Phan Van Truong, or Truong and Quoc may have written the points together. Quoc did, however, physically deliver the message to the papers. The eight points were clearly outlined:

(1) general amnesty for all native political prisoners;

(2) reform of Indochinese justice by granting the natives the same judicial guarantees as were enjoyed by Europeans;

(3) freedom of press and opinion;

(4) freedom of association;

(5) freedom of emigration and foreign travel;

(6) freedom of instruction and the creation in all provinces of technical and professional schools for indigenous people;

(7) replacement of rule by decree by rule of law;

(8) election of permanent Vietnamese delegation to the French Parliament, to keep it informed of the wishes of indigenous people.[7]

were not going to work, maybe an uprising through war was the way to unification. ⟶

Wilson's Fourteen Points

At the Paris Peace Conference in 1919, Wilson presented his Fourteen Points plan for peace, which was previously read to the US Congress. When Quoc heard the points, he thought the president would be sympathetic to the cause of Vietnamese independence from colonialism. Points V and XIV specifically addressed colonial questions and the rights of occupied nations. But Wilson refused to meet with Quoc. The plan was also not well received by the French or the British, who disagreed with certain provisions.

*Quoc had a talent for writing powerful articles and letters
and moving speeches.*

French police, wary of his antigovernment activity,
tracked Quoc's every move while he lived in Paris.

PARISIAN PROTESTER

uoc spent the next few years in Paris,
living there until 1923. He built alliances
in political organizations and wrote propaganda
materials. After Quoc had so publicly made demands
on behalf of the Vietnamese people at the Paris Peace

Conference, the French government began logging his activities. The Sûreté, France's police force, kept track of Quoc. Members waited outside his apartment and followed him around Paris whenever he left his home.

QUOC'S ROOMMATES

Quoc shared this apartment with two other revolutionaries: Phan Van Truong, a friend and mentor, and Phan Chu Trinh, a scholar. Both men were much older than Quoc and had been jailed for subversive activities. Quoc felt that being jailed was an acceptable part of the life of a revolutionary.

The French government sent spies to listen in on Quoc's circle of comrades. In one conversation, the two older revolutionaries, though they had carried out protest bombings in the past, said they believed in making more peaceful

Marxism-Leninism

The Marxism-Leninism theory led to the Russian revolution in November 1917. The three main leaders of the revolution were Vladimir Lenin, Joseph Stalin, and Leon Trotsky. Quoc studied these theories at length in order to incorporate them into the revolution he hoped to create in Vietnam.

demands for freedom in the future. Quoc did not agree. He believed that if war and bloodshed were required, then that is what the Vietnamese should do to gain independence. But Trinh disagreed, asking, "What do you want our unarmed countrymen [to do] against the Europeans and their weapons?. . . Why should people die uselessly without any result?"[1]

The two men also disagreed on the benefits of French colonialism. Trinh thought the French were helping modernize Vietnam. Quoc did not trust the French or their motives. Despite their

Man of Many Aliases

Many revolutionaries have used aliases because they risked being jailed or killed for going against their governments. Ho was no exception. Some reports stated that he had as many as 75 different names over his lifetime, while some say the number was closer to 50. Some of his names are better known than others. These include his birth name of Nguyen Sinh Cung and Nguyen Tat Thanh, which was the name given to him according to Vietnamese tradition. When he left Vietnam in 1911 on the French passenger ship, he went by the name of Van Ba, and he officially changed his name to Nguyen Ai Quoc while in Paris. Finally, in 1941, he reentered Vietnam and changed his name to Ho Chi Minh in 1942. There are various translations of Ho Chi Minh, but roughly it means "He Who Enlightens."[2]

Ho's siblings stated that he had an accident as a child that caused the upper portion of his left ear to be scarred. This unique feature enabled French security forces to later put the aliases together to see that certain named men were, in fact, all one man: the revolutionary leader Ho Chi Minh.

disagreements, Trinh and Quoc remained friends and respected each other.

But Quoc continued to distrust the French. In part, this was because the French intercepted messages and newspapers he tried to send back to his homeland, which he hoped would result in a revolution. This caused problems in trying to gain the people's support for an uprising.

FOUNDING MEMBER OF THE FRENCH COMMUNIST PARTY

At the close of the Paris Peace Conference in 1920, Quoc had spoken with various politicians who did not even know where Indochina or Vietnam was. Quoc realized, "We need to make a lot of noise in order to become known."[3] So, Quoc continued attending political meetings and passing out his eight-point program to attendees. He also wrote *Les Opprimés*, a book about the

Condemning Colonialism

Around 1920, Quoc asked the following question in political debates with those who opposed the ideas of the Russian revolutionary Vladimir Lenin: "If you do not condemn colonialism, if you do not side with the colonial people, what kind of revolution are you waging?"[4] Lenin was a Marxist. A Marxist is interested in creating a classless Communist society. Quoc had studied Lenin's writings over the years and idolized him.

French dealings in Indochina. But Quoc did not
have a publisher or the money to publish the book
himself.

In the summer of 1920, Quoc was hospitalized
for an abscess on his right shoulder. Then, he lost
his job in the photograph shop because his employer
thought the shoulder injury was an early indication
of tuberculosis. Quoc did have tuberculosis later in
life, but it is not clear if he actually was showing signs
of it at this point.

In November 1920, Quoc and a comrade went to
a meeting of the Socialist Revolutionary Party. Quoc
also attended a meeting of the Soviets' Committee
for the Third International, or Comintern. The
groups at these meetings discussed what was to be
done to unite their causes. They wanted more rights
for the working classes. They wondered whether they
should join the much more radical Soviet parties.
The groups feared their approach thus far had not
been rebellious enough to get results. They hoped to
learn from Communist uprisings around the world.

On December 24, 1920, Quoc traveled to
Tours, France, and gave a speech at the Congress
of the Socialist Revolutionary Party. Because he was
at the conference, he became one of the French

Signs promoting communism were hung in the Communist office in Paris.
Quoc was a vocal founding member of the French Communist Party,
speaking out on behalf of the French-oppressed Vietnamese.

Communist Party's founding members. In his
speech that day, Quoc summed up the crimes of
French colonialism in Vietnam:

> But behind the three colours of liberty, equality and
> fraternity, France introduces alcohol, opium and prostitution
> to all of her colonies and sows misery, ruin and death along
> with her ill-gotten riches.[5]

The speech was well received by the other delegates
to the meeting. Afterward, several people shouted,
"Down with the colonial sharks!"[6]

CONFLICTS

In the winter of 1921, Quoc was in the hospital
for two weeks having his shoulder abscess removed.
Once treatment was completed, he left without
paying the hospital, claiming he had no funds.
In addition to money shortages and health issues,
Quoc's apartment mates complained that Quoc
was too radical. They felt his presence increased the
police's monitoring of their group. With money
short, Quoc and his comrades could not pay the
rent. Finally, Quoc and Trinh moved. In order to
afford the new place, Quoc went back to working
as a photograph retoucher, which lessened the time
he had for politics and writing. That summer,
informers reported heated arguments coming from
the new apartment. Within a few months, Trinh
moved away.

Quoc also received criticism of his revolutionary
efforts. He had sent a copy of his eight-point
program to the Human Rights League, a French
group. In November 1921, Quoc received a letter
from an official there named Gabriel Seailles.
Seailles wrote, "Your proposals are formulated in
too general a manner. It would be in your interest to
communicate your complaints with more precision."[7]

Quoc was also getting criticism from Phan Chu Trinh, his mentor and former roommate. Trinh pointed out that Quoc was writing for a more elite and educated audience, but the people he needed to reach were the poorer Vietnamese laborers who were less educated. In February 1922, Trinh wrote a letter to Quoc, trying to convince him to change his approach. In the letter, Trinh wrote,

I am an exhausted horse who can no longer gallop; you are a fiery stallion. . . . But I am writing this letter because I hope you will listen and prepare your grand design. . . . Following your method you have sent articles to the press here to incite our compatriots to mobilize their energy and spirit. But this is vain. Because our compatriots can't read French or even [quoc-ngu]; they are incapable of understanding your articles![8]

Trinh was being critical, but he was trying to be encouraging and wanted

Quoc the Playwright

In 1922, in his anger at colonial rule, Quoc wrote a play called *The Bamboo Dragon*, which ridicules the Emperor of Annam. The play was performed in the Paris suburb of Garches at a festival sponsored by a newspaper Quoc often wrote for: *L'Humanité*. Journalist Léo Poldès liked the play and reviewed it, stating, "Carefully crafted, animated by a certain Aristophanic verve and not lacking in scenic qualities."[9] At this time in his life, Quoc wrote extensively in various genres. All of his writing focused on political propaganda.

Quoc to succeed in his revolutionary efforts.

Later, Quoc did heed the advice of his old friend and mentor. By 1922, Quoc had made connections with several newspapers. In May 1923, Quoc started his own newspaper called *Vietnam Hon*, which means "the soul of Vietnam." Quoc hoped to reach the masses of poorer Vietnamese with this newspaper. The bimonthly publication would be written in quoc-ngu. But the first issue of *Vietnam Hon* was printed without its founder, because on June 13, 1923, Quoc disappeared from Paris.

*Quoc at the Congress of the Socialist Revolutionary Party,
Tours, France, December 1920*

During his time in Moscow, Quoc studied the theories of Marx and Lenin and planned his revolution for Vietnam.

REVOLUTIONARY ABROAD

fter disappearing from Paris, Quoc appeared in Moscow, Russia, later in the summer of 1923. When Quoc left Paris, he took a series of bus, train, and boat rides to keep away from Parisian security. A comrade gave him a fake passport, and Quoc disguised himself as a successful businessman.

Quoc always remained a nationalist fighting for Vietnam, but now he was looking at the international aspects of defeating colonialism in oppressed nations. The global perspective had advantages because Quoc could work with other colonized nations fighting for independence. In addition to being a strong nationalist, Quoc had also become a committed Communist. He thought communism provided the best means of achieving independence and organizing Vietnamese society.

Conferences and Meetings

Quoc attended conferences and traveled secretly throughout Russia, China, and France. Quoc initially went to Russia because he was invited to attend the International Peasant Conference, a political conference, on October 10, 1923. At the meeting, Quoc lobbied against having French colonials in Vietnam, explaining how the French were exploiting the peasants in his homeland. He stated that the French were exhibiting a form of racism and slavery. In keeping with his focus, Quoc criticized the Comintern for its failure to act in addressing the colonial question. He wrote a letter to the French Communist Party criticizing the Comintern, stating that its written goals "have served, so far, only to decorate the paper they were written on."[1] Quoc also requested meetings with the president of the Comintern, but his requests were ignored.

In 1924, Quoc attended the Fifth Comintern Congress in Russia. He used his language skills and worked as a translator for the Soviets. After this, Quoc wanted to go on a mission to China, but his plans were delayed for months because of the Chinese civil war (1920–1937). On November 11, 1924, Quoc finally traveled to Canton, China.

Through these meetings Quoc was growing a network of international support from countries that surrounded Indochina. He was becoming known as a leader and not just a propagandist. He had

Death of Lenin

On January 21, 1924, Russian revolutionary Lenin died. Quoc was deeply saddened by this loss, especially because meeting Lenin was one of the reasons he had traveled to Moscow. Now, he would never meet his hero of Russia's revolution. In the book *People and Revolution*, Lenin wrote, "A people's insurrection and a people's revolution are not only natural but inevitable."[2]

worked his way into important political circles in Russia, China, and France with the goal of spreading Communist ideas and sympathy and support for colonial peoples.

Recruiting and Training the Thanh Nien

In Canton, Quoc worked closely with exiled Vietnamese people as a translator. After studying the problems in China, Quoc determined, as biographer Truong Chinh wrote,

> *The assassination of this or that governor could not overthrow the colonial regime or lead the revolution to victory . . . a strong political party was needed, which would organize the masses.*[3]

With this concluded, in 1925 Quoc organized the Thanh Nien (Association of Vietnamese Revolutionary Youth), whose members attended a training program for young revolutionaries. They would learn about communism and be trained to fight. The group's numbers grew quickly because so many young people had grown up in poverty and were angry with the government. Each class was made up of only approximately 20 students.

The tradition of the *Thanh Nien* continues in Vietnam through the Vietnam National Youth Federation, which publishes the newspaper *Thanh Nien*.

Betraying a Friend

As Quoc become more involved in his cause, it became clear that he would go to any length to gain independence for his people and to secure the triumph of his own leadership of the anticolonial movement. According to David Halberstam's biography *Ho*, in 1925, the Vietnamese revolutionary became worried that his friend Phan Boi Chau was hampering progress of the movement with his old, stifling ideas. Quoc and his comrades decided to turn Chau over to the French police. That way, the French would have a scapegoat and feel like they had done something to thwart the revolution. Also, Quoc could remove Chau as his competition for leadership of the uprising. Quoc thought that having such a public figure arrested would also draw attention to the anticolonial cause.

In a letter, Quoc invited Chau to Canton to attend meetings about nationalism. However, when Chau got to the train station in Shanghai, he was arrested immediately. Quoc was paid a large ransom for setting up the operation, while the French police sentenced Chau to life in prison and hard labor. The French pardoned and released Chau a few weeks later because of civil unrest and protesting. Quoc later justified his actions with several points:

    a. *Phan Boi Chau, as an influential nationalist leader, would be a dangerous rival to the Communists in their scheme to control the anti-French movement;*

The Thanh Nien Program

Quoc was the main instructor of the Thanh Nien and also wrote the Communist manual used in teaching. In *Ho Chi Minh: The Missing Years*, Sophie Quinn-Judge reported that he taught the students "human evolution, world geography, and Vietnamese history to Marxism-Leninism, Sun Yatsen's Three Peoples' Principles, and Gandhian non-violence."[4]

Many of the students came from the province of Annam, where Quoc was born. Some reports say that three classes had graduated from the program and a fourth class had started when the program dissolved in April 1927. Other books claim the number of graduating classes was much higher.

b.   *The ransom money would be used for a just cause, [that is] the promotion of Communism;*

c.   *The arrest, trial, and execution of Phan Boi Chau would arouse the Vietnamese people against the French rule and intensify the spirit of revolution.*[5]

THE THANH NIEN DISBANDED

In 1927, anticommunist sentiment from Chiang Kai-shek's regime in China led to the dissolution of the Thanh Nien. The young trainees returned home to Vietnam. Now spread across Vietnam, many of the young trainees started other revolutionary cells.

However, there was dissent among even the Vietnamese who wanted revolution. As a result, three separate Communist parties were formed. Eventually, the central committee in Hong Kong contacted Quoc. The group wanted him to bring the three splinter groups together for a unified revolution. If the groups stayed separate, Quoc feared that no one's party would gain prominence. Instead, the groups would either keep fighting against each other or dissipate.

FOUNDING THE INDOCHINESE COMMUNIST PARTY

Since Quoc was not yet able to reenter Vietnam without arrest and possible execution for his activism, he held a meeting in Hong Kong. For lack of a better place, the revolutionaries met in the stands of a Hong Kong soccer stadium during a soccer game. The noise of the cheering crowd was advantageous when Quoc and his comrades wanted to discuss revolution without being overheard by authorities. Quoc brought many of the splintered-off groups back into one unified party.

Quoc's Marriages

There is much debate over whether Quoc ever married. According to a biography by Pierre Brocheux, on October 18, 1926, Quoc married Tang Tuyet Minh. Quoc was going by the name Ly Thuy at the time. He was 36 and the bride was 21. A biography by William J. Duiker reported that Quoc fled Canton on May 5, 1927, leaving his wife there, just before police raided his home. He had tried to convert her political beliefs to his own but was unsuccessful. He was alleged to have fathered one daughter during the marriage.

Duiker reported that in 1931, Quoc started seeing a colleague in Hong Kong named Nguyen Thi Minh Khai. At times, she was referred to as his wife, but there is no evidence the couple ever married. She was arrested by British police in Hong Kong for her political activism.

The debate over Quoc's personal life comes from the fact that he was enshrined into legend by his people after his death. Thinking of him as a mortal man who married tarnishes that legendary vision. Leaders at the time of Quoc's death painted him as a legend and created and upheld the myth that he had always been a single man.

"1. To overthrow French imperialism, feudalism and the reactionary Vietnamese capitalist class.

2. To make Vietnam completely independent.

3. To establish a government composed of workers, peasants and soldiers.

4. To confiscate the banks and other enterprises belonging to the imperialists and put them under control of the government.

5. To confiscate all of the plantations and property belonging to the imperialists and the Vietnamese reactionary capitalist class, and distribute them to the poor peasants.

6. To implement the eight hour working day.

7. To abolish public loans and the poll tax. To waive unjust taxes . . . .

8. To bring back all freedom to the masses.

9. To carry out universal education.

10. To implement equality between man and woman."[6]

　　　—Goals for the ICP

On February 3, 1930, Quoc founded the Indochinese Communist Party (ICP).

The Indochinese Communist Party, which Quoc founded in 1930,
met secretly for years to strategize Vietnam's uprising.

Fed up with longtime French oppression, Vietnamese peasants staged revolts in 1930, leading to chaos and many deaths.

STUDYING ABROAD

fter the ICP was founded in 1930, Quoc traveled in Russia, China, and other countries as a covert international agent for the Comintern, spreading its ideas across borders. As the 1930s dawned, smaller uprisings spread through Vietnam, and many revolutionaries were arrested. Quoc found himself dodging arrests and punishments from those inside and outside of his alliances.

Peasant Uprisings

In early 1930, the peasants in Vietnam held uprisings against the French colonialists. At the time, Quoc was still in Hong Kong, so he was not directly involved. There were many strikes, including in rubber plants and weaving mills. Through the strikes, the peasants wanted to accomplish three things: better wages, lower salt prices, and elimination of district taxes.

On September 12, 1930, in one strike, protestors marched through villages and asked people to join them. The protest grew and soon 5,000 to 6,000 people were marching. But, the French dropped bombs on the marchers, causing the people to scatter. The bombs killed 200 protestors. Later, people returned to bury the dead, but the French mistook this return for a second protest and dropped more bombs. Another 15 people died. Mass graves were created along the road for those who had been killed.

The price of the combined revolts was high: a reported 10,000 Vietnamese died and another 50,000 were imprisoned. The protests went on for two years. Quoc learned of these unsuccessful uprisings. He knew he would have to wait for the right time to strike in order for his revolution to succeed.

Revolutionary Arrests

The French worried about a real revolution because so many peasants were now becoming involved that their sheer

Con Son Island Prison

Con Son, also known as Poulo Con-dore, was a famous island prison in southern Vietnam. The prison was 50 miles (80 km) from shore. In 1970, *Time* magazine wrote an article featuring the prison. The article included reports from US officials who toured Con Son and saw the famed tiger cages, which were 5-foot (1.5-m) by 9-foot (2.7-m) cells that each housed three prisoners. Although Quoc was never imprisoned there, by 1970, many of the top North Vietnamese officials had at one time been imprisoned at Con Son.

Later, in an interview, Vietnamese Prime Minister Pham Van Dong commented about the time he spent at Con Son in the 1930s:

I must say that the penal island of Con Son as well as many other prisons in our country at that time were places where the French colonialists exiled and killed untold numbers of our revolutionary fighters. But we must also see the other side to this. The prisons were schools, were places where revolutionary combatants trained themselves in every way. . . . Under extremely poor and harsh conditions, we had the complete works of Lenin accepted by the prison post office and transferred to us by the prison guards who sympathized with us.[1]

numbers could overpower the French. So, the French arrested several top officials in the ICP, including future leader Pham Van Dong and Quoc's secretary-general, Tran Phu, who was tortured and died in prison. The French were unable to arrest Quoc, however, because he was in China. They sentenced him to death in his absence. The sentence caused Quoc to continue living abroad in hiding.

On June 6, 1931, Quoc was arrested in a British territory in Hong Kong. The French wanted Quoc extradited, but he was not turned over to the French because he was considered a political refugee. While in prison, Quoc's health declined. He had tuberculosis and was moved to the prison hospital. Rumors about Quoc's whereabouts stirred again. There was even a memorial service held in Moscow because his comrades there believed he had died in prison.

In 1932, Quoc escaped from the prison hospital with the help of British sympathizer Frank Loseby, an anti-imperialism activist. Loseby got Quoc on a ship headed for Shanghai. Once there, Quoc tried to make contact with his allies in Russia and the Comintern, but he had to wait. At one point, he sought refuge as a monk until it was time to leave.

Quoc eventually communicated with his comrades and reentered Moscow.

Studying Leninism and Marxism in Moscow

At about this same time, Russia's Communist leader, Joseph Stalin, began his reign over the Soviet Union. Stalin eliminated many other Communist leaders who debated with him. However, Stalin did not kill Quoc during this time of upheaval. Quoc was loyal to Stalin and not seen as a threat to the dictator. Quoc spent several years hiding in Moscow and studying at the Lenin School, whose students were promising young leaders. Though there is dispute about whether Quoc actually studied there, experts have stated that his tactics as a revolutionary reflect the Communist values of the school, proving he did study there.

The ICP Questions Loyalty of Comrade Quoc

By April 1935, some ICP members were losing trust in Quoc. The ICP blamed Quoc and his policies for security lapses, which led to the arrests of more than 100 members of the Thanh Nien. Additionally, some thought Quoc showed too

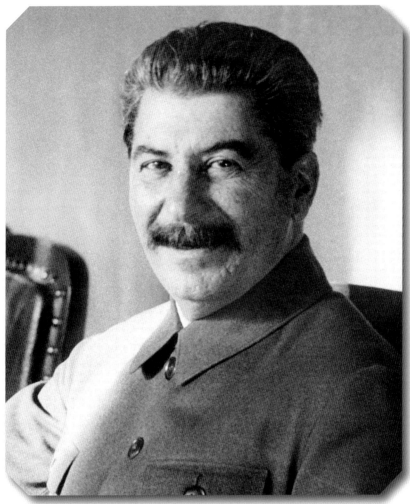

A believer in Stalin's points of view, Quoc visited Russia often as he grew into a significant Communist leader himself.

many nationalist tendencies. One report included complaints that he was not even a Communist before 1930. This brought forth questions about his loyalty to the Communist Party. Another report said he was taking advantage of the ICP for his own ends. These complaints, along with Stalin's purging of people he mistrusted, caused division within the ICP.

Quoc argued that the ICP was not doing enough for colonial people. Additionally, he wanted to recruit more than workers and peasants. He believed that a broader front would be more effective for revolution. When the Seventh Comintern Congress finally met on July 25, 1935, Quoc was not selected as an agent for the Comintern. Debate about how to punish Quoc for possibly causing the security leaks in the Thanh Nien included expulsion from the Communist Party and death. However, neither of these sentences was carried out. Quoc remained in Moscow and, as punishment, studied communism for at least two more years.

SETTING THE STAGE FOR INDEPENDENCE

In 1938, Quoc was reunited in China with his old friend Pham Van Dong. He was also introduced to Vo Nguyen Giap, a former history instructor and Communist activist. By the time they met, Giap had been reading Quoc's writing for many years. Giap commented that he was surprised Quoc had retained his accent from central Vietnam after being gone for so long. From 1938 to 1940, Quoc remained in China and worked with Giap and Dong. While in China, Giap studied guerrilla warfare tactics.

By this time, Europe and parts of the Pacific were fighting in World War II (1939–1945). On June 22, 1940, France surrendered to Germany. Quoc recognized that this defeat would change things in French-occupied Indochina. The Japanese also took advantage of this weakness and moved troops into Vietnam and set up bases there in late September 1940.

After this, Quoc wanted to move forward, but first he thought the ICP should change its party affiliation so that anticommunist sentiment would not harm their cause for an independent Vietnam. The new party was called Viet Nam Doc Lap Dong Minh Hoi, or League for the

Vo Nguyen Giap

Beginning in the 1940s, Vo Nguyen Giap became a general of armies that supported the Vietminh. From the beginning of World War II through the fall of Saigon in 1975, Giap led Quoc's Vietminh armies in Vietnam. This four-star general was known for his surprise attacks on enemies and for exploiting their weaknesses. Giap's most famous battles against France included a Christmas Eve attack in 1944 and the Battle of Dien Bien Phu in 1954. In 1968, he led the Tet Offensive against the United States.

Independence of Vietnam. Later, Quoc suggested a shortened version, so the name Vietminh was adopted. The new Vietminh Party's stance was to be labeled as nationalist rather than as Communist in order to gain more support from the Vietnamese people. However, this angered neighboring Communist Chinese leaders. By 1941, it was time for Quoc, now in his fifties, to finally return to Vietnam. ⌐

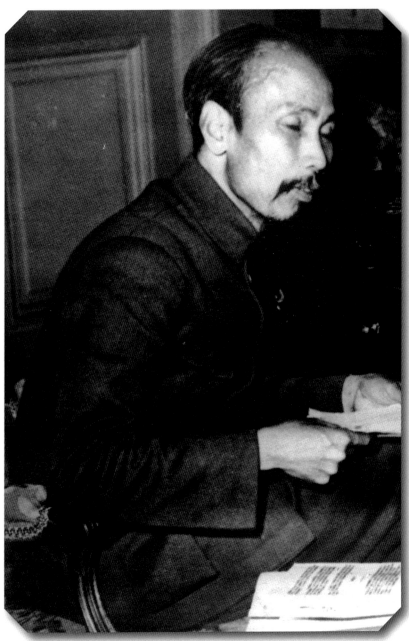

A global citizen with many aliases,
Quoc finally decided to return home to Vietnam in 1941.

*Quoc's Vietnam homecoming was closely preceded
by the entrance of oppressive Japanese troops.*

COMING HOME

On February 8, 1941, for the first time in
30 years, Quoc returned to Vietnam. He
was accompanied by Vo Nguyen Giap and Pham Van
Dong. When the men crossed the Chinese border
into Tonkin, the northern region of Vietnam, Quoc

kissed the Vietnamese soil. The men would remain in hiding, strategizing in a limestone mountain cave. The hideout was known as the cave at Pac Bo. Here, Quoc established his new headquarters. He named surrounding monuments, dubbing a nearby creek Lenin Stream and a mountain Karl Marx Peak. Outside of the caves, the trio built a hut from branches and a table from bamboo. Quoc lived at Pac Bo for one year.

Quoc asserted that assassination of enemy leaders was not the way of real revolution. Instead, he emphasized that change must come from organizing and educating the people. Patience should be valued above all. They must wait until the time was right. Some premature uprisings had been attempted as recently as September 1940 in Tonkin and January 1941 in Nghe An Province. Quoc's success later could be attributed to this focus and ability to wait for revolution instead of hurrying into disorganized rebellion and failing as others had failed.

On Choosing Communism

Charles Fenn, a US intelligence officer, interviewed Ho in 1945 and asked him why communism was Ho's political choice for Vietnam. Ho answered, "To gain independence from a great power like France is a formidable task. . . . One doesn't in fact gain independence by throwing bombs and such. That was the mistake the early revolutionaries all too often made. One must gain it through organization, propaganda, training, and discipline. One also needs . . . a set of beliefs, a gospel, a practical analysis, you might even say a bible. Marxism-Leninism gave me that framework."[1]

Japan Rules

In August 1940, the colonial French who ruled northern Vietnam had allowed Japan to set up military operations there during World War II. But the French essentially became a puppet administration while the Japanese were really in control. At first, many Vietnamese thought the Japanese would free them from French colonial rule. They volunteered to fight with the Japanese. However, it soon became clear that the Japanese intended to rule Vietnam.

Meanwhile, the new Vietminh Party quickly gained powerful allies who gave money to aid its cause. These included the French Resistance under Charles de Gaulle operating with some French forces in Vietnam. The French Resistance aided the Allies in World War II and opposed the German occupation of France. During this initial forming of the Vietminh, the American Office of Strategic Services, which later became the CIA, also provided support to the Vietnamese because the United States wanted to defeat the Japanese who occupied northern Vietnam.

Arrested in China

In July 1942, Quoc returned to China to meet Nationalist Chinese leader Chiang Kai-shek and gain

Chiang Kai-shek, who imprisoned Ho for more than a year

support against the Japanese. He also wanted to meet
with the Chinese Communist Party to explain why the
Vietminh had chosen to use a nationalist front rather

than a Communist one. When he left for China, Quoc adopted a new name to help him disassociate from any Communist parties for which Nguyen Ai Quoc had been notorious. The new name was Ho Chi Minh.

Not long after Ho entered China, he was arrested by the Kuomintang, the Chinese nationalist party. He was arrested because the Vietminh Party conflicted with the goals of the Kuomintang, which was already establishing a Vietnamese party in China called the Dong Minh Hoi.

For 13 months, the Chinese kept Ho imprisoned. During this time, he was shuffled between several prisons. Rumors spread that he had died. Ho's comrades grieved and even had a funeral. While imprisoned, Ho somehow sent a poetic note handwritten on newspaper to his comrades: "The clouds are setting the peaks aglow / The peaks are hugging the clouds— / I wander alone, roused to feeling, / Scanning the distant southern sky: / I am thinking of my friends."[2] Giap read the note and recognized Ho's handwriting immediately. He knew Ho was alive.

Though Ho was alive, the harsh conditions of the prison did make him ill with tuberculosis again. Finally, Chinese General Chang Fa-kwei secretly summoned Ho. In exchange for Ho's release, Chang asked Ho to spy on the French and Japanese for China. Chang would also put Ho in charge of the Dong Minh Hoi in China. World War II was still raging, and the intelligence reports, if Ho could acquire them, could prove invaluable in the war effort. The two men struck a deal, and Ho was released. Chang also contributed $100,000 monthly to the Vietminh to thwart Japanese war efforts.

On the long journey back to his Vietminh headquarters, Ho was ill and delirious. He seemed to be reciting his last wishes, which stayed focused on his goals as always: "We must at all costs seize independence. We must be ready for any sacrifice, even if the entire chain of the Central Mountains must catch fire."[3] Fortunately, Ho was given quinine and sulfa medicine, which may have helped him recover more quickly.

Prison Poetry

Over the many months that Ho was in prison in 1942, he wrote several poems. These poems were later published in a collection titled *Prison Diary*. Oddly enough, he wrote the poems in classical Chinese rather than in his native language.

Ho's earlier poems in prison seemed to have more hope: "It is your body which is in prison, not your mind."[4] Later, he wrote of prison conditions affecting his health: "Four inhuman months / in the depths of this jail. / More than ten years' aging / Has ravaged my body!"[5]

Guerrilla War Training

During Ho's time in jail and over the rest of 1942 and 1943, members of the Vietminh were trained in guerrilla war tactics in Liuchow, China. Giap became a general who would lead the troops. These troops were made up of small groups of Vietnamese who used techniques such as sabotage to surprise the enemy. This element of surprise became a trademark tactic of the Vietminh guerrilla armies. Still, the main concern voiced by Ho's comrades in staging an uprising, even with the guerrilla armies, was that they had no weapons. Ho simply responded, "Capture enemy arms to kill the enemy."[6]

Time for Action

On March 9, 1945, the Japanese attacked the French and took control of Vietnam. Ho assessed this as a positive turn of events because he

Guerrilla Warfare

Chinese leader Mao Zedong provided Quoc's most immediate example of guerrilla warfare. However, guerrilla warfare had been practiced previously by others, including the Scots under William Wallace and the Americans under George Washington. Mao stressed that a nation with inferior weapons against an enemy should especially use these tactics. Additionally, climate, society, and terrain are things an oppressed nation can use to its advantage against its oppressor. The military effort of guerrilla warfare must also work in conjunction with political goals or it will fail. Quoc's soldiers under General Giap's direction studied guerrilla tactics at the Liuchow war school in China.

knew his Vietminh forces were more powerful than
the Japanese. He believed the Vietnamese would
be able to defeat the Japanese more easily than they
could have defeated
the French. By July,
Giap urged Ho that
the time to act was
now, but Ho had
always been one to
wait. Ho's strategy
was based on the
teachings of Lenin,
which embraced
two things: wait for
the most "favorable
moment," and
focus on the "main
adversary."[7]

In early August,
that favorable
moment appeared.
The United States
attacked the
Japanese cities of
Hiroshima and

Gaining the People's Support

By 1945, several unsuccessful uprisings had
already taken place in Vietnam. Ho explained
three critical things that needed to take place
for a successful revolution: "(a) the enemy must
be in an untenable position; (b) the people
must be clearly conscious of oppression; (c)
the revolutionaries must have finished prepar-
ing the ground."[8]

One way Ho accomplished the second
objective was through journalism. He published a newspaper during this time called
Independent Vietnam.

Many years later, in a 1981 interview, Prime
Minister Pham Van Dong explained how Ho
had accomplished the third objective of organizing the Vietminh and gaining support from
the Vietnamese people:

> After the establishment of the Viet Minh
> Front . . . virtually everybody had become
> members of the various National Salva-
> tion organizations . . . for workers, for
> peasants, for women, for senior citizens
> and for young people. It was through this
> . . . that Comrade Vo Nguyen Giap, I and
> many other comrades were able to create
> a military base area . . . . which led to the
> success of the August Revolution.[9]

Nagasaki by dropping atomic bombs with devastating consequences. The Japanese surrendered to the United States soon after. This timing and the weakening of the Japanese was the opportunity Ho had been waiting for to take over military bases the Japanese had set up in Vietnam. On August 14, the Vietminh overtook Japanese-occupied villages across Vietnam. This event became known as the August Revolutions.

"When guerrillas engage a stronger enemy, they with-draw when he advances; harass him when he stops; strike him when he is weary; pursue him when he withdraws."[10]

—*Mao Zedong, Chinese Communist leader, On Guerrilla Warfare*

On September 2, Ho gave his famous "Declaration of Independence" speech in Ba Dinh Square in the center of Hanoi. In this speech, Ho declared himself the first president of Vietnam. ⌐

The infamous bombing of Hiroshima, Japan, created an opening
for Vietnam to take back control from weakened Japan.

*Ho, second from left, in France
with French President Georges Bidault, 1946*

STEADFAST
WAR STRATEGIST

fter Ho gave his historic "Declaration of Independence" speech on September 2, 1945, he still had a long fight ahead for his people. The French were not ready to give up resource-rich Vietnam. Ho would make some decisions in the conflict against the French that would frustrate his supporters.

First Indochina War

On September 25, the French tried again to reassert control over Vietnam. Eventually, the Vietnamese and the French tried to negotiate. In 1946, the French flew Ho to Paris for peace talks. At the peace talks, Ho agreed to let the French set up a temporary government in South Vietnam, while Ho retained control of North Vietnam as the first Democratic Republic of Vietnam (DRV) president. The North became a liberated zone, or area that was free from colonial rule. Many Vietnamese called Ho a traitor for making this concession. Ho defended his stance, saying it was a short-term solution that would lead to long-term independence for Vietnam.

But France soon wanted its colonial interests back. A war between the French and the Vietminh broke out on December 19, 1946. This was the First Indochina War. It was fought mostly in North Vietnam.

Initially, the Vietminh lost thousands of soldiers because of the superior French weaponry. The French also had support from some Vietnamese who did not want a Communist government and opposed the Vietminh. But Ho was steadfast and willing to lose the lives of his countrymen to achieve Vietnamese independence. He was often quoted as saying, "You would kill ten of my men for every one I killed of yours. But even at that rate you would be unable to hold out, and victory would go to me."[1]

HELP FROM CHINA

By 1949, Ho achieved an alliance with China and the new government headed by Communist Mao Zedong. After that, China supplied the Vietminh with weapons to fight the French. China was the first foreign government to acknowledge Ho as the legitimate leader of all of Vietnam. With Chinese support secured, the Vietminh's main strategy was to wear down the French in a long war. Though the French were winning in terms of the number of soldier casualties and battles, the Vietminh would not give up. The strategy worked and, eventually, public opinion and support for the French waned as the conflict dragged on.

Beginning in 1950, the American Office of Strategic Services, which had been helpful to Ho against the Japanese during World War II, turned its support to the French colonials. US President Harry S. Truman feared that communism would spread across Asia if the Vietminh took over all of Vietnam.

VICTORY AT DIEN BIEN PHU

In 1954, the Geneva Conference was scheduled to take place that July in Switzerland. The conference had two main goals: unify Korea and reestablish peace in Indochina. This impending conference put pressure on the French to end the fighting in Vietnam.

Before the conference, the French planned to win the Battle of Dien Bien Phu, a valley in northwestern Vietnam. The French did not think they would need many troops to battle the Vietminh, which had lost thousands in previous battles. So, the French left many of their troops guarding other outposts in Vietnam. On March 13, the Vietminh

Ho the Autobiographer

In the 1940s and the 1950s, Ho wrote two biographies about himself under aliases. One of the aliases was Tran Dan Tien. Writing the books under these assumed names allowed Ho to write in third person about himself and to talk up his accomplishments without sounding like he was bragging. He was also able to control what was said about him by doing the writing himself. In writing the accounts, he was creating a legend for himself by getting people to read and talk about him.

The Battle of Dien Bien Phu, First Indochina War, 1954

attacked with many more troops than expected and overwhelmed the French. The Vietminh also had powerful artillery supplied by the Soviets, which the

French also did not expect. After a two-month siege, the Vietminh claimed victory on May 7. As a result of the victory, Ho and the French entered into peace talks at the Geneva Conference.

Geneva Conference

On July 21, peace agreements were signed, and Vietnam was now officially split at the seventeenth parallel into two zones—Communist North Vietnam, known as the Democratic Republic of Vietnam (DRV), and noncommunist South Vietnam, known as the Republic of Vietnam. Ho was in charge of North Vietnam. Bao Dai, who had been the emperor of Vietnam until 1945, was put in charge of South Vietnam.

As part of the agreements, presidential elections were scheduled to be held in 1956. After those, the northern and southern regions of Vietnam would become unified as one country under a ruler chosen by the people. In 1955, the United States feared communism. So, the United States helped set up a noncommunist government in South Vietnam led by anticommunist Ngo Dinh Diem. However, when it came time for the 1956 elections, Diem, with US support, refused to participate because, he argued, the Communists would not allow a fair election to take place.

In addition to canceling the elections, Diem's government took control of communal land, which villages had traditionally governed. This angered the people and many joined the Viet Cong (VC), a Communist-led secret guerrilla force in South Vietnam. By 1960, the VC grew to approximately 10,000 members and threatened to overthrow Diem's government. In 1960, the National Liberation Front (NLF) was founded and replaced Ho's Vietminh. The NLF concentrated its efforts in South Vietnam.

In 1961, US President John F. Kennedy increased support for Diem and South Vietnam. In May 1963, Diem, a Catholic, supported an operation against Buddhist monks, in which many were killed and arrested. Kennedy asked Diem

Communal Land

In Vietnam, communal land was owned by a village. The land could be divided in two ways: rented out by a landlord to needy people or split among various social groups. The renters paid for the land use by trading services rather than paying in money. On the land, peasants grew various crops, but the most important crop was rice. Rice exports under French rule were at an all time high, while reports indicated that a third of the Vietnamese people were starving for lack of food. Landlords got rich renting the tenant-occupied farms, particularly in the Mekong delta where rice was plentiful. All the while, the peasants remained poor.

Ngo Dinh Diem

to improve relations with the monks, but Diem
refused. In response, Kennedy shifted US support
to leaders who opposed and eventually killed
Diem. After that, leadership in South Vietnam

rotated, which resulted in political unrest. The chaos provided another opportunity for the VC, which gained control of a large majority of the population by 1964.

THE VIETNAM WAR

After President Kennedy was assassinated in November 1963, Vice President Lyndon B. Johnson was sworn in as president of the United States. On August 2, 1964, the US warship *Maddox* was fired upon by a torpedo in the Gulf of Tonkin. It was believed that the North Vietnamese had fired on the ship. Johnson warned the North Vietnamese that another attack would bring retaliation.

On August 4, Johnson reported another torpedo attack on two US destroyer ships in the Gulf of Tonkin, though there was speculation over whether the second attack actually occurred.

"The war may still last 10, 20 years or longer. Hanoi, Haiphong and other cities and enterprises may be destroyed, but the Vietnamese people will not be intimidated!"[2]

—*Ho Chi Minh, 1966*

Because of the second attack, Johnson requested that Congress grant him authority to increase involvement in Vietnam. Congress approved the request. Though no declaration of war was ever made, the first US ground troops entered Vietnam in March 1965. This led the United States into a long conflict with Vietnam, known to Americans as the Vietnam War and to Vietnamese as the American War.

WEARING DOWN THE ENEMY

When US troops began fighting in Vietnam,

Napalm

During World War II, on July 23, 1944, the first use of napalm was reported. It was also used by the Allies in several other battles against Japan, Germany, Korea, Vietnam, and possibly in much more recent wars. Napalm-B bombs, a variation of the original napalm, were one of the weapons the United States used against North Vietnam.

Napalm is a powder that becomes a military weapon when mixed with liquid gasoline. Napalm bombs cause a lack of oxygen, which makes breathing difficult. Those exposed to the bombs become incapacitated. They are also burned. When napalm strikes a person's skin, it is unbearably painful, layers of skin peel off, and second-degree burns leave widespread scarring and can also damage nerves and motor skills.

The napalm bombs used during the Vietnam War were made by filling 165-gallon (624.6-L) containers with the jellied substance and then dropping the containers from planes onto a targeted area. One bomb could damage 2,500 square yards (2,286 sq m). The most well-known producer of napalm was Dow Chemical Company. In 1969, a film titled *Inextinguishable Fire* by Harun Farocki brought attention to the company, as did public demonstrations against the company. It stopped producing napalm in 1969.

Americans thought they would win quickly. They were not prepared to be engaged in a long, drawn-out struggle. From 1963 to 1969, while Johnson was president of the United States, he and Ho attempted negotiations through exchanged letters. Johnson was looking for compromise, but Ho was steadfast in his determination for his people's goal of independence as a Communist nation.

US soldiers wade through a stream in South Vietnam.

Ho was fiercely determined to gain Vietnam's independence.

LEGENDARY LEADER

H o was determined not to lose the war against the United States, especially when his country was so close to gaining independence. On January 30, 1968, General Giap began a surprise attack called the Tet Offensive in an attempt to create a general uprising of the South Vietnamese people and end the war quickly.

THE TET OFFENSIVE

The attack began one day before the Vietnamese holiday of Tet, which celebrates the Lunar New Year. It was supposed to be a time of cease-fire.

The Tet Offensive occurred in Saigon, Hué, and hundreds of other cities and villages in South Vietnam from the seventeenth parallel to the Mekong delta—even the US Embassy. Though the attack of 84,000 North Vietnamese Army (NVA) and VC troops was a surprise to the United States, the fighting and the overall outcome were not a success. In fact, 58,000 of those troops died, while only 3,400 US and Army of the Republic of Vietnam (ARVN), South Vietnam's army, soldiers were killed or wounded.

The popular uprising Ho had hoped for in the South did not happen, but the Tet Offensive was successful in that Johnson's will to continue was shaken. The illusion that the United States was winning the war was also shattered because these battles were described in the media as a stalemate.

Withdrawal of US Troops

Battle of Two Leaders

In 1965, Ho explained why he thought the United States would not stop the war in Vietnam in an interview with a British correspondent. Ho said, "It's the old question of saving America's face. But, you know, the door is quite open. They can leave at any time. Once they decide to go, we will do all we can to help them. We will even lay out the red carpet."[1]

But Johnson would not admit defeat so easily. Johnson said, "America wins the wars that she undertakes. Make no mistake about it."[2]

In March, Johnson announced in a television speech that he would not seek reelection. The military requested 206,000 more US troops be sent to Vietnam, but Johnson declined this request and approved only 30,500 for economic reasons as much as public opinion. Johnson said peace talks would start in Paris in May. Johnson's actions did not strongly affect US public opinion, which showed steady decline in support for the war. The peace talks failed and the new US president, Richard M. Nixon, began gradually withdrawing troops in July 1969.

Ho's Later Years

Ho was now 79 years old. His comrades wanted him to slow down, but Ho disregarded their pleas and continued holding military strategy meetings. Though he had been so steadfast in waging war and putting the lives of Vietnamese at risk, he did show that he wanted some relief for the people. He instructed his comrades that once a peace settlement was reached, the Vietnamese people should have their agricultural taxes forgiven for one year as a thank you from the government for the people's sacrifice during the war.

Ho Chi Minh Dies

On September 2, 1969, at 9:45 a.m., Ho Chi Minh died of a heart attack in Hanoi. It was the twenty-fourth anniversary of Ho's reading of the Declaration of Independence, a national holiday. The Communist leaders did not want to interrupt the holiday celebrations, so they waited until September 3 to announce Ho's death. Because of this, September 3 is the official date listed for Ho's death. When the news spread to the rest of the world, the North Vietnamese people received 22,000 messages of condolence from 121 countries. There was, however, no comment from the US government, which was still entrenched in the war. The funeral for Ho was held on September 8 and was attended by 100,000 people.

Ho's Wishes

In Ho's will, first drafted in 1965, he wrote of wanting independence for his people, a better

Ho's funeral on September 9, 1969

standard of living for them, and equality among the sexes. In death as in life, his final testament stayed focused on his revolutionary vision.

Ho wanted to be cremated. He did not want the money of his countrymen spent on elaborate ceremonies or memorials. He said, "Not only is cremation good from the point of view of hygiene, but it also saves farmland."[3] He had requested that his ashes be scattered amid three Vietnamese mountains, but this wish was not carried out. Instead, just the opposite occurred. Ho was idolized and memorialized. His body was embalmed and placed on display in a huge granite mausoleum in Ba Dinh Square.

SHRINE FOR A LEGEND

Before the memorial was constructed, models were set up around the country and suggestions solicited from Ho's people. A committee received more than 30,000 suggestions. In December 1971, plans for the memorial moved forward.

First US President Visits Vietnam

In 2000, Bill Clinton was the first US president to set foot on Vietnamese soil since the war ended in 1975. The people of Vietnam greeted Clinton positively when he visited Hanoi. The visit was not announced widely, nor was it kept a secret. The president gave a half-hour speech that was televised and translated into Vietnamese. He said he was "conscious that the histories of our two nations are deeply intertwined in ways that are both a source of pain for generations that came before, and a source of promise for generations yet to come."[4]

The final version of the shrine was enormous, with thick columns that towered over the square. The design is similar to other shrines to Communist leaders, including Lenin's Tomb in Moscow. Engraved lettering above the columns reads simply *Chu Tich Ho Chi Minh*, or "President Ho Chi Minh." Ho's body was placed in a glass coffin that is housed in the shrine. People can view Ho's body when they visit the shrine. Today, more than 15,000 people a week wait in line to visit the embalmed leader.

Reeducation Camps and the Boat People

After the fall of Saigon, the people of South Vietnam who had not supported Ho's Communist-led revolution were subject to retaliation by the new government in the form of prison camps known as reeducation camps. Hundreds of thousands of people were sent to these camps, including former military leaders, politicians, and other educated South Vietnamese. The camps were used to punish and repress the South Vietnamese. The Vietnamese government defended the camps saying the detainees were war criminals who needed to be indoctrinated into Communist thinking. Prisoners were forced to write confessions to war crimes, including the smallest infraction against North Vietnam. The new government also enacted population resettlement, a program in which people were forced to relocate to other areas of the country to better distribute the population.

Many people fled Vietnam to seek refuge in other countries. They left by helicopter, land, and plane, but mostly by boat. These people were known as boat people. The first boat people totaled at least 131,000 people. Approximately half of the initial wave of boat people died from disease, starvation, and other plights on their way to find refuge. Some were taken in by countries they approached, while others were turned away.

Independence at Last for Ho's People

Ho never saw a unified Vietnam, but the North Vietnamese continued to fight to realize his dream. A peace agreement between the United States and North Vietnam was officially reached in Paris on January 27, 1973. The last US troops left Vietnam by helicopter on March 29, 1973.

The fighting in Vietnam between the NVA and VC and the ARVN continued for two more years. On April 30, 1975, North Vietnamese troops overtook South Vietnam's capital of Saigon, ending the war. Saigon was renamed Ho Chi Minh City in honor of the tireless leader. Though he was not there to see it, there was independence at last for Ho's people.

Ho's Legacy

Now deified as a national figure for independence, Ho remains as

Ho Chi Minh City

Ho Chi Minh City is the largest city in Vietnam and a popular tourist destination. The climate is warm and humid. Half of the year, known as the monsoon season, is rainy, with the most rain falling May through October. The other half of the year is dry.

Vietnam Today

Traveling to Vietnam today may surprise tourists because the country has many modern conveniences from Western culture. Though Vietnam is still Communist, free market abounds. In large cities such as Ho Chi Minh City and Hanoi, Internet cafés line the streets, car drivers honk horns to warn pedestrians to move out of the way, and the bustling pace creates a familiar feel of modernization. In 2011, the population of Vietnam was estimated to be more than 90 million, and the average age was nearly 28. The population had a high literacy rate of 90.3 percent. The biggest crop produced was still rice.

much a mystery in death as he was in life. His writings and his style of leadership live on in his publications. But perhaps Ho's real legacy lies in the triumph of the people who stood up against large enemies and gained their independence. ⌐

*Ho's ultimate dream of an independent Vietnam
was finally achieved six years after his death.*

TIMELINE

1890

On May 19,
Ho Chi Minh is born
as Nguyen Sinh Cung.

1901

Cung's mother dies.
Following Vietnamese
custom, Cung's
father selects a new
name for his son:
Nguyen Tat Thanh.

1911

Thanh leaves Vietnam
as a crewmember
on the *Amiral
Latouche-Tréville* on
June 5. He becomes
a cook's apprentice.

1919

Quoc represents
Vietnamese interests
at the Paris Peace
Conference in France,
but he is not able to
speak with
US President Wilson.

1924

Quoc attends
the Fifth Comintern
Congress.

1925

Quoc trains
young revolutionaries
who are members
of the Thanh Nien.

1913

Thanh visits the United States and lives in New York City's Harlem neighborhood.

1913

Thanh moves to London, England, and joins the Overseas Workers' Association.

1917

Thanh moves to Paris, France, where he officially changes his name to Nguyen Ai Quoc and becomes a political activist.

1930

On February 3, Quoc founds the Indochinese Communist Party.

1931

Quoc is arrested in Hong Kong on June 6.

1932

Quoc escapes from prison with help from Frank Loseby, a British activist. He studies at the Lenin School in Moscow.

TIMELINE

1941

Quoc returns to Vietnam. He founds the Vietminh in Pac Bo and operates his hidden headquarters in a nearby mountain cave.

1942

Quoc takes a new name: Ho Chi Minh. On August 17, he is imprisoned in China.

1943

On September 10, Ho is released from prison.

1960

Ho establishes the National Liberation Front. This takes the place of the Vietminh.

1965

US President Lyndon Johnson sends marines as first ground troops into South Vietnam on March 6.

1969

On September 2, at age 79, Ho dies of a heart attack in Hanoi.

1945	1946	1954
Ho reads the Declaration of Independence for Vietnam on September 2.	Ho signs an agreement with France for independence, but it does not last. By December, war starts between the French and the Vietminh.	In July, the Geneva Accords split Vietnam into two: the noncommunist South and the Communist North.

1973	1975	1975
The last US ground troops leave Vietnam on March 29.	On April 30, the North Vietnamese take over Saigon, the capital city of South Vietnam. Vietnam finally declares independence.	Saigon is renamed Ho Chi Minh City on May 1.

Essential Facts

Date of Birth

May 19, 1890

Place of Birth

Kim Lien, Annam Province, Vietnam

Date of Death

September 2, 1969

Parents

Nguyen Sinh Sac and Hoang Thi Loan

Education

Quoc Hoc School; Lenin School

Marriage

Tang Tuyet Minh (1927)

Children

Ho allegedly had one daughter with Tang, but this has never been proven.

CAREER HIGHLIGHTS

In 1919, Ho was selected by his comrades to represent them at the Paris Peace Conference. On February 3, 1930, he founded the Indochinese Communist Party. On September 2, 1945, Ho gave his famous "Declaration of Independence" speech in Ba Dinh Square in Hanoi, North Vietnam, to a crowd of more than 500,000 people. Ho led his people in fighting several enemies in his pursuit of unification for Vietnam. He fought the Japanese occupation of Vietnam during World War II; the French colonials for almost eight years, until the Battle of Dien Bien Phu; and the Americans and South Vietnamese, who opposed Ho's Communist-led North Vietnam.

SOCIETAL CONTRIBUTION

Ho spent his entire life trying to help Vietnam gain independence from colonialism and to unify. This dream was realized in 1975, six years after his death. Ho continues to be idolized by the Vietnamese for his nationalism and charisma.

CONFLICTS

Ho was imprisoned twice for revolutionary activities. He believed in independence and unification for Vietnam at any cost. Ho continued to practice communism for his country, though he recognized its downfalls. Over the course of the Vietnam War, approximately 3.4 million Vietnamese, 75,000 French, and 58,000 Americans died. Countless others were affected.

QUOTE

"The war may still last 10, 20 years or longer. Hanoi, Haiphong and other cities and enterprises may be destroyed, but the Vietnamese people will not be intimidated!"—*Ho Chi Minh*

Glossary

assassinate
To secretly kill someone, usually a politician or public figure.

colonialism
When one nation maintains control or power over another country or its people.

communal land
Property owned collectively by a community instead of by an individual.

communism
A governmental system in which property is owned by the country, community, or one political party that regulates all economic activity of a people.

dissent
Difference or disagreement in opinion, usually with a government or politics.

extradite
To turn over a criminal to another country.

guerrilla warfare
Irregular warfare often used by a member of an independent group against a ruling army or government.

imperialism
A country ruling over another nation or colony to serve its own interests and increase its own empire.

Indochina
Area of Asia consisting of Burma, Cambodia, Laos, Thailand, Vietnam, and West Malaysia.

nationalism
Loyalty or patriotism toward one's own country.

negotiation
Discussion used to reach agreement between parties.

refugee
Someone who seeks a safe place to live away from his or her own country, often in times of war.

revolutionary
One who goes against or tries to change the established way.

splinter group
A group that breaks away from a larger group to form its own faction, usually political or religious.

territory
Land belonging to a country or under its control.

untenable
Not able to be defended in an attack.

Viet Cong
Military name for the Communist-led guerrilla army of South Vietnam during the Vietnam War era.

Vietminh
Military name for the Communist-led army of North Vietnam under the direction of Ho Chi Minh during the Vietnam War era.

ADDITIONAL RESOURCES

SELECTED BIBLIOGRAPHY

Brocheux, Pierre. Claire Duiker, trans. *Ho Chi Minh: A Biography*. New York: Cambridge UP, 2007. Print.

Duiker, William J. *Ho Chi Minh*. New York: Hyperion, 2000. Print.

Fall, Bernard B., ed. *Ho Chi Minh, On Revolution: Selected Writings, 1920–66*. New York: Frederick A. Praeger, 1967. Print.

Halberstam, David. *Ho*. Lanham, MD: Rowman & Littlefield, 2007. Print.

Lacouture, Jean. *Ho Chi Minh*. Paris: Editions du Seuil, 1967. Translated by Peter Wiles as *Ho Chi Minh: A Political Biography*. New York: Random House, 1968. Print.

Lawrence, Mark Atwood. *The Vietnam War: A Concise International History*. New York: Oxford UP, 2008. Print.

Quinn-Judge, Sophie. *Ho Chi Minh: The Missing Years, 1919–1941*. Berkeley: U of California P, 2002. Print.

FURTHER READINGS

Caputo, Philip. *10,000 Days of Thunder: A History of the Vietnam War*. New York: Atheneum, 2005. Print.

Edelman, Rob. *The Vietnam War*. Farmington Hills, MI: Blackbirch, 2003. Print.

Warren, Andrea. *Escape from Saigon: How a Vietnam War Orphan Became an American Boy*. New York: Farrar, 2004. Print.

Wiest, Andrew. *The Vietnam War: 1956–1975*. Oxford: Osprey, 2002. Print.

Web Links

To learn more about Ho Chi Minh, visit ABDO Publishing Company online at **www.abdopublishing.com**. Web sites about Ho Chi Minh are featured on our Book Links page. These links are routinely monitored and updated to provide the most current information available.

Places to Visit

Ba Dinh Square
Center of Ba Dinh, Hanoi, Vietnam
This was the location of Ho's famous speech declaring independence for Vietnam. A huge granite mausoleum there holds Ho's preserved body. Tourists wait in line daily to pay their respects.

Ho Chi Minh Museum
Duong Nguyen Tat Thanh, District 4, Ho Chi Minh City, Vietnam
84-8-829-9749
This museum was built in the 1990s and shows the life of Ho Chi Minh through artifacts.

Vietnam Veterans Memorial
900 Ohio Drive Southwest, Washington, DC 20242
202-426-6841
www.thewall-usa.com
Completed in 1982, the Vietnam Veterans Memorial was created to honor all US veterans who served in Vietnam. In addition to a long wall that lists the names of those who perished in the war, there are two statues honoring those who served, including nurses.

SOURCE NOTES

Chapter 1. Fight for Independence

1. Bernard B. Fall, ed. *Ho Chi Minh, On Revolution: Selected Writings, 1920-66.* New York: Frederick A. Praeger, 1967. Print. 143.

2. Ibid.

3. Ch'u Chai and Winberg Chai. *Confucianism.* Hauppauge, NY: Barron's Educational Series, 1973. Print. 36.

4. Henry Kamm. *Dragon Ascending: Vietnam and the Vietnamese.* New York: Arcade, 1996. Print. 3.

Chapter 2. Revolutionary Start

1. Pierre Brocheux. *Ho Chi Minh: A Biography.* Trans. Claire Duiker. New York: Cambridge UP, 2007. Print. 3.

2. William J. Duiker. *Ho Chi Minh: A Life.* New York: Hyperion, 2000. Print. 32.

3. Ibid. 33.

4. Pierre Brocheux. *Ho Chi Minh: A Biography.* Trans. Claire Duiker. New York: Cambridge UP, 2007. Print. 6.

5. William J. Duiker. *Ho Chi Minh: A Life.* New York: Hyperion, 2000. Print. 41.

Chapter 3. Seeing the World

1. William J. Duiker. *Ho Chi Minh: A Life.* New York: Hyperion, 2000. Print. 47.

2. Ibid.

3. Bernard B. Fall, editor. *Ho Chi Minh, On Revolution: Selected Writings, 1920-66.* New York: Frederick A. Praeger, 1967. Print. 43.

4. William J. Duiker. *Ho Chi Minh: A Life.* New York: Hyperion, 2000. Print. 45.

5. Pierre Brocheux. *Ho Chi Minh: A Biography.* Trans. Claire Duiker. New York: Cambridge UP, 2007. Print. 12.

6. Ibid.

7. Sophie Quinn-Judge. *Ho Chi Minh: The Missing Years, 1919–1941.* Berkeley: U of California P, 2002. Print. 12.

Chapter 4. Parisian Protester

1. Sophie Quinn-Judge. *Ho Chi Minh: The Missing Years, 1919–1941.* Berkeley: U of California P, 2002. Print. 17.

2. William J. Duiker. *Ho Chi Minh: A Life*. New York: Hyperion, 2000. Print. 248.

3. Sophie Quinn-Judge. *Ho Chi Minh: The Missing Years, 1919–1941*. Berkeley: U of California P, 2002. Print. 29.

4. David Halberstam. *Ho*. Lanham, MD: Rowman & Littlefield, 2007. Print. 39.

5. Sophie Quinn-Judge. *Ho Chi Minh: The Missing Years, 1919–1941*. Berkeley: U of California P, 2002. Print. 32.

6. Ibid.

7. Ibid. 37.

8. Ibid. 38.

9. Pierre Brocheux. *Ho Chi Minh: A Biography*. Trans. Claire Duiker. New York: Cambridge UP, 2007. Print. 19–20.

10. David Halberstam. *Ho*. Lanham, MD: Rowman & Littlefield, 2007. Print. 30.

Chapter 5. Revolutionary Abroad

1. Pierre Brocheux. *Ho Chi Minh: A Biography*. Trans. Claire Duiker. New York: Cambridge UP, 2007. Print. 25.

2. Mao Tse-tung. "On Guerrilla Warfare: What is Guerrilla Warfare?" *Marxist.org*. Maoist Documentation Project, 2000. Web. 13 Jan. 2011.

3. N. Khac Huyen. *Vision Accomplished? The Enigma of Ho Chi Minh*. New York: Macmillan, 1971. Print. 26.

4. Sophie Quinn-Judge. *Ho Chi Minh: The Missing Years, 1919–1941*. Berkeley: U of California P, 2002. Print. 98.

5. N. Khac Huyen. *Vision Accomplished? The Enigma of Ho Chi Minh*. New York: Macmillan, 1971. Print. 28.

6. David Halberstam. *Ho*. Lanham, MD: Rowman & Littlefield, 2007. Print. 52–53.

Chapter 6. Studying Abroad

1. "Interview with Pham Van Dong, 1981." *Vietnam: A Television History*. WGBH Educational Foundation, 19 Feb. 1981. Web. 13 Jan. 2011.

Source Notes Continued

Chapter 7. Coming Home

1. William J. Duiker. *Ho Chi Minh*. New York: Hyperion, 2000. Print. 570.

2. Jean Lacouture. *Ho Chi Minh: A Political Biography*. Trans. Peter Wiles. New York: Random House, 1968. Print. 79.

3. William J. Duiker. *Ho Chi Minh: A Life*. New York: Hyperion, 2000. Print. 302.

4. Jean Lacouture. *Ho Chi Minh: A Political Biography*. Trans. Peter Wiles. New York: Random House, 1968. Print. 81.

5. Ibid. 82.

6. N. Khac Huyen. *Vision Accomplished? The Enigma of Ho Chi Minh*. New York: Macmillan, 1971. Print. 50.

7. Jean Lacouture. *Ho Chi Minh: A Political Biography*. Trans. Peter Wiles. New York: Random House, 1968. Print. 101.

8. Ibid. 93.

9. "Interview with Pham Van Dong, 1981." *Vietnam: A Television History*. WGBH Educational Foundation, 19 Feb 1981. Web. 13 Jan 2011.

10. Mao Tse-tung. "On Guerrilla Warfare: What is Guerrilla Warfare?" *Marxist.org*. Maoist Documentation Project, 2000. Web. 13 Jan. 2011.

Chapter 8. Steadfast War Strategist

1. Jean Lacouture. *Ho Chi Minh: A Political Biography*. Trans. Peter Wiles. New York: Random House, 1968. Print. 171.

2. "Reflections and Opinions of President Ho Chi Minh." *New York Times*. 4 Sep. 1969. Print. 16.

Chapter 9. Legendary Leader

1. "Reflections and Opinions of President Ho Chi Minh." *New York Times* 4 Sep. 1969: Print. 16.

2. *The Fog of War: Eleven Lessons from the Life of Robert S. McNamara*. Errol Morris, Dir. Sony Pictures Classics, 2003. Film. 1:16:33.

3. "American Experience: Return with Honor: People & Events: Ho Chi Minh." *PBS*. PBS Online, 1999–2000. Web. 13 Jan. 2011.

4. David E. Sanger. "Clinton in Vietnam: The Overview: Huge Crowd in Hanoi for Clinton, Who Speaks of 'Shared Suffering.'" *New York Times* 18 Nov. 2000. Print. 1.

INDEX

INDEX CONTINUED

ABOUT THE AUTHOR

Kristin F. Johnson teaches writing and lives in Minnesota. Johnson has won several writing awards, including the Loose-leaf Poetry Series Award, the Loft's Shabo Award, and the Mystery Writers of America Helen McCloy Award.

PHOTO CREDITS

AP Images, cover, 3, 29, 64, 67, 74, 78, 86, 96; AFP/Getty Images, 6, 23, 33, 43, 53, 95, 99 (top, bottom); VNA/AP Images, 11; LAM/AP Images, 13; Rob Broek/iStockphoto, 14; Frederic Soreau/Photolibrary, 17; Keystone-France/Gamma-Keystone/Getty Images, 24, 34, 39, 89, 97 (top), 98; Archive Photos/Photolibrary, 44; HOANG DINH NAM/AFP/Getty Images, 48; The Print Collector/Photolibrary, 54; James Abbe/AP Images, 59; Popperfoto/Getty Images, 63, 97 (bottom); George R. Caron/AP Images, 73; Howard Sochurek/Time & Life Pictures/Getty Images, 81; Horst Faas/AP Images, 85